"And He has said to me, 'My grace is sufficient for you, for power is perfected in weakness.' Most gladly therefore, I will rather boast in my weaknesses, so that the power in Christ may dwell in me."

2 Corinthians 12:9

Also by Barbara Mcgreger:

The Last Mile Home: Ordinary Insights from an Extraordinary God

This book aims to teach readers that God is everywhere and works through everything and anything. We just have to look for Him—even in the little things.

Covered and Smothered: Devotionals for Whatever Life Brings Your Way

Does God hear us, feel us in our time of need? Does He send messages and blessings through the most ordinary things? I believe He does, and He is able to be discovered in everything we go through and everything we face, even in the things we think He wouldn't trouble Himself with, if we just look for Him.

BUT GRACE PREVAILED

A Mother's Story of God's Forgiveness, Mercy, and Healing

Barbara McGreger

Rogersville, Alabama

First Edition

But Grace Prevailed

Author: Barbara McGreger
© 2013 by Eleos Press www.eleospress.com

All rights reserved.

This book or parts thereof may not be reproduced in any form, stored in a retrieval system, or transmitted in any form by any means without prior written permission of the author, except as provided by United States of America copyright law.

Cover Art: W. Scott Moore
Cover Design: createspace™ and W. Scott Moore
Interior Formatting: Eleos Press www.eleospress.com
Also available in eBook form

Unless otherwise noted, all "Scripture quotations taken from the New American Standard Bible®, Copyright © 1960, 1962, 1963, 1968, 1971, 1972, 1973, 1975, 1977, 1995 by The Lockman Foundation. Used by permission." (www.Lockman.org)

Eleos Press publishes this volume as a document of critical, theological, historical, and/or literary significance and does not necessarily endorse or promote all the views or statements made herein, or verify the accuracy of any statements made by the Author. References to persons or incidents herein may have been changed to protect the identity of those involved.

ISBN-13: 978-0615901671

PRINTED IN THE UNITED STATES OF AMERICA

Matt's Preface

We've talked for years about writing our story. Mom wrote most of it when I got out of high school. As she's finished this book, we've talked a lot about what's happened to us and what we've been through. I think it's a great idea to tell our story, because it's really God's story of what He's done. I'm proud that we've been through it all, and what we've accomplished with God's help. I'm glad we're alive!

Mom has told me about how sick I was when I was first born—we were—and very close to death. And how God let us live in spite of what everyone said about us and what the doctors and all those people said about me. I feel great, and blessed, and thankful about it all. If we didn't have the bad, we wouldn't have all the good things to tell. So we gotta tell the bad, so everyone can know how we got to the good and how good God has been to us and for us.

She told me about a dream she had once. She dreamed a doctor came to her and told her he could make all the damage to my brain all healed and make me normal—but there was a catch: the catch was that, if the surgery were done, I wouldn't be able to remember all the things that had happened before the surgery and all the ways God has healed me. She asked me if a doctor could really do that would I have the surgery, and I said, "NO." I told her I knew normal people, and I'm glad I'm not normal (ha ha ha). I told her I never wanted to forget how much God has done for me and what we've been through.

I'm proud of us and proud of God no matter what anyone else thinks. I hope you're blessed by our story.

Matt McCurry
Wednesday, October 9, 2013

Foreword

Recently I had the privilege of seeing a Rolls Royce Phantom up close. This car made everyone who set eyes on it almost speechless. I heard someone say, "This Rolls is the car of cars." After admiring this vehicle intimately for several minutes, it was almost impossible to keep from turning around to catch another glimpse as I walked away.

Later I did some research on the Rolls. I quickly learned that I had simply seen the glory of a finished product. I had no clue what all transpired behind the scenes days and even months before some metal and assorted parts became a Rolls Royce Phantom. I didn't know it took an entire day to make a radiator and five additional hours to polish it by hand. I didn't know it took 800 man hours to make the body of this awesome vehicle. While I enjoyed the Phantom's glory, I didn't know its story.

I feel the same way about the author of this book, Barbara McGreger, and her bright, witty, and smiling son named Matt. On the surface, Barbara is just, as she put it, a "good ole' gal" who loves her Lord, loves her son beyond comparison, and loves people. To know Barbara is to know a picture and pillar of strength, fortitude, faith, and faithfulness. To know Matt is to know a young man who loves affection, loves to give affection, loves people, and certainly loves his mother. However, I'm afraid that while most of us share in Barbara and Matt's glory, we don't understand their story.

Throughout the pages of this book, Barbara does a masterful job of intimately testifying of the miracle-working power of God. She brings us very close to her and Matt during some very trying and troubling times that, quite frankly, are hard to fathom. This book will break your heart as you feel as if you're living a mother's nightmare with Barbara. Then the book will piece your heart back together and bring a joyful smile to your face as you see God working in the lives of Matt and Barbara. In the end, we'll celebrate who these two wonderful people are more than ever because we'll have an inside view of what they experienced to get to where they are today.

Friend, if you've ever thought that Barbara and Matt have been a blessing to you, just take a moment and really engross yourself into the pages of this book. It's one thing to celebrate someone's glory. It's another thing to celebrate someone's glory after having been informed and inspired by someone's story. You'll never view Barbara and Matt the same way again. After reading this book, their words will take on a different tone with you. You'll also find their smiles will tug at your heart just a little more. Then you'll be like me and the Rolls Royce—you'll continue to have the need for "one more glimpse" of a blessed mother and child named Barbara and Matt.

Antoyne L. Green, Senior Pastor
New Life Baptist Church
Athens, Alabama

Table of Contents

MATT'S PREFACE I

FOREWORD III

DEDICATION V

INTRODUCTION VII

A "POSITIVE" IN ALL THE NEGATIVE 1

SURPRISE...NO SURPRISE 5

REPEATING WHAT I HATED MOST 7

HOW DID I GET HERE? 9

ANGELS 13

WADDLING THROUGH 17

READY FOR BABY, BABY NOT READY 21

THE ARRIVAL 29

THE BEGINNING...OR THE END? 31

THE TRUTH ABOUT TRUTH 39

CONFIRMATION 43

JUST A PEEK OF REALITY 47

FAMILY PLAYS FAMILY 51

-PHOTO ALBUM- 53

CONFRONTATION OF TRUTH 63

THE FIRST (AND MAYBE LAST) ENCOUNTER 67

THE CHANGE 75

NOW WHAT? 79

BEGINNINGS 81

NORMAL ISN'T HERE 85

MY NEW NORMAL 89

CHOICES, LIFE OR DEATH 91

GIVING HIM UP 95

GOD, DID YOU HEAR ME? 99

LIFE GOES ON 105

"MONSIE" 111

GROWING INTO OUR "NORMAL" 113

THE LOST GIRL IS FOUND 119

LIFE WORTH LIVING 121

Dedication

This book is dedicated to JESUS CHRIST: My Lord, YOU have made *__THE__* difference in my life. Why you saved me, I'll never understand. Your love I'll never fully grasp. I love you. Thank you for loving me and never leaving me.

To Joel Nelms, and a host of others whom I call my "angels," those (I believe) who were strategically placed in my life by Almighty God to keep me safe, to love me as best they could, and to see me through some mighty rough times. (I'd name all of you but I'd be afraid I'd leave one out by accident and that would break my heart!) I trust I've told you who you are to me, how much I love you and how grateful I am to you.

To Hew Smith, Dara Evans, Carol Romine, Cecilia Jackson (especially you & unnamed others) for seeing in Matt what no one else saw, for fighting for him and giving him chances and opportunities. What a difference you made in his life...and mine. How could I ever thank you?

To those who were there from the beginning, I wonder if you have any idea how much I love you, and how grateful I am to you for your imprint on our lives.

Introduction

I understand why a lot of people don't want to share their stories. It's gut-wrenching, embarrassing and very, very humbling. It's good, it's bad, and it's scary. I've been so blessed to not only survive but *thrive* without having been discovered dead in a ditch or a multitude of other not-so-pretty scenarios. I feel I must share ours as I believe most of what happens to us can be used to help someone else *if we choose to share it*. I could have so easily become a sad statistic, and I should have. God allowed us to live through it all, so the least I can do is share it hoping it will help someone else.

For the longest time, I thought it was my son's story only and I tried to keep myself out of it. However recently, having had the pleasure of sharing small fragments of what God has done in my life with women across the Southeastern United States via Stonecroft Ministries as well as independently, I've come to realize many women (and even some men) have had similar experiences. I feel I have no choice but to tell it, ugly and all.

There are many sides to a story, and all those involved will see things differently. This is *my* recollection of the events included, how *I* remember things and how *I* felt. This isn't my Mom's story, my father's story, my ex-husband's story. This is my perspective of what happened and how I felt through my childhood and when I had my son. Others involved may not remember it like I do, so if offended, my apologies.

-Barbie-

A "POSITIVE" IN ALL THE NEGATIVE

Congratulations, me! I've earned another title. This one, I'm sure, will be my crown, the one I'm remembered by: an *unwed mother*. It could be worse, I guess. I'm not a teenager. Nobody's responsible for me but me. Wait. I think that makes it worse. This one will show. No hiding or explaining it away. This one's different all right. Life-alteringly different.

I couldn't help but remember, once again, the words of my aunt all those years ago: *"Bless her heart, she doesn't have a chance. She'll never be nothin'."* She nailed it. I have proved her right with every self-destroying trophy. I know them well, I've kept an up-to-date inventory and remind myself all the time of all my milestones. Every single mistake, bad choice, bad word, bad boy, bad everything. Bad *me*.

I considered myself a bona fide "lost cause" since I heard those words when I was six. When my parents divorced back in the 60s, it wasn't the widely accepted "norm" it is now. Not only that, there were no resources available like today. People treated us differently because of the stigma attached. My younger sister took it hard. She was Daddy's girl so she had a hard time being away from him. I was the older sister, so I felt I needed to step up and put my own feelings aside for her sake as well as Mom's. I was one mad, depressed, and sad little girl who kept her feelings well hidden from everyone else.

I don't remember many details surrounding that time but what I do remember is the sadness. Mom was sad, and I'm surely scared to death. How she must've felt having to go back home divorced, and start all over again. She was never the same. My little sister cried for Dad all the time. Everyone tried their best to make her happy and soothe her. It would work for a little while, and then she'd go back to being heartbreakingly sad and missing her Dad. I didn't want anyone to see me cry so I didn't unless I was sure no one was around. I didn't want to be anything else to deal with; it was miserable enough.

My sister eventually decided to live with Dad, Eventually, Mom and I got an apartment. She went back to school and took classes during the day and worked at night which meant I was by myself. It didn't take long before everyone knew it and at the ripe old age of 12, our apartment was a haven for anyone who didn't want to go home. After 10:00 p.m. when Mom worked I was a very popular girl and anything you wanted could be found at my house. That's when I started drinking and smoking pot. I was the official party girl of our area.

My poor mother. The things I put her through. This was not her fault. She was doing the best she could to keep a roof over our heads in addition to dealing with her own pain and trying to better her life (and her income) by going to school. She couldn't have possibly known the scope of what was going on with me though she knew I had changed and was "into something." Her main concern was our safety. She, herself, told all my friends to stay at our house. She didn't want anyone drinking and driving. My friends called her "Mom" because she fed them, took care of them and treated them with the same love she did me. Often, she'd come home from working all night and had to step over people to get to her room to go to bed. Where we would be without her, I shudder to think. She and I had our arguments and moments, but she was always there for me no matter what I did. I couldn't help but wonder how she would react to this news. She didn't like my boyfriend and, at the time I got pregnant, I don't think she really liked the person I was. Frankly, I didn't either!

Now this: pregnant, 23 years old, pretty much living with my boyfriend. I had to tell him, my family, and my bosses. What would they say? What would they think?

SURPRISE...NO SURPRISE

From my earliest memories, I wore sadness and fear like everyday clothes. As I grew up, I found happiness in jobs, being around friends and having a good time. I made friends easily because I was the life of the party. I had several different jobs. I'd stick with something until I got bored or unhappy, and then move on. Finding a job never was a problem.

I couldn't help but wonder how that would change since I was pregnant. Guess it was time to settle down and be responsible. After all, I was going to be a mother. Wow. A Mom.

I told my boyfriend, Mom and sister about the pregnancy. I don't think anyone was surprised. I think they were all just waiting for my next mess-up. She asked if we were going to get married and I told her no. In my mind, two wrongs didn't make a right. Realistically neither of us was ready for marriage. He was still in school and pretty wild. I was too, but all of that stopped the moment I got pregnant. That was the first time in my life I ever followed all the rules and did everything by the book. I felt my life was a mess, but I wasn't going to mess up my child's life. None of this was the baby's fault. Why in the world would someone like me be allowed to have a baby? None of it made any sense. I knew girls who had intimate relationships with every guy they dated and this never happened to them. I wasn't like that! Why me? Why him? Why now?

Then again, why *not* me? The words spoken by my aunt had become my truth. I believed I was never going to amount to anything but throwing a baby into the mix was a little over the top. Part of me felt like that sad little girl and the other was the angry expecting-everything-to-be-tragic-woman I had become. Poor kid. Poor baby.

REPEATING WHAT I HATED MOST

Growing up, our lives were so different from everyone else I knew. Everyone's two-parent home had a father who worked and a mom who stayed at home. Everyone was "normal" except for us. We, in my mind, were far from it and I hated that. We were outcasts, not invited to parties and sleep-overs. I felt everything in my life was affected by the fact that my parents were divorced.

Here I was, making the "abnormal" choice for my unborn child to raise him in the same atmosphere with one exception. How I was raised wasn't my mother's choice. How my son would be raised would be 100% my choice. It was all on me.

Was this my payback for being so bad? Would my child do the things I had done?

My boyfriend and I had come to terms with the pregnancy. We moved in together for a little while but with him in school with apparently a lot of debt he moved back in with his parents and I moved in with Mom.

To say the least things were strained all the way around. He was very supportive but I knew he didn't want a family. He was still sewing his wild oats and I was trying my best to be a good pregnant person. Mom and my sister were very supportive but I felt they were ashamed of me, at the least, an embarrassment. I couldn't see how I could make any of this work.

I surely got a good sense of how Mom felt when my parents divorced. She wasn't working when that happened. At least I had a job and supported myself just fine and I knew I would find a way to take care of my baby. Nevertheless, it was daunting to say the least. So many emotions consumed me: fear, happiness, fear, joy, fear. How would all this work out? I just couldn't wrap my head around taking care of someone else; I wasn't that great at taking care of myself!

HOW DID I GET HERE?

While in school, the band was a sanctuary for me. I think had I not had it, I would have dropped out. It was the only thing I was good at. My main instrument was the clarinet, and I played well enough to try out for First Chair. Eventually, I got it. I loved every part of it. The summer before my senior year, I tried out for Drum Major and got that, too. That was surprising to me as I was still drinking and partying as often as I could. I had progressed to laying out of school with my partying friends and relatives. My only ambition for high school was to graduate and get out. That's it. I had a chance for a scholarship but, as I was convinced that I would only ruin that and make a fool out of myself, I didn't pursue it.

As my belly grew, my love for the child I carried did too. How I could care so much for someone I had never seen was beyond my comprehension. Those closest to me said I was born to be a mother. Maybe I was. I was looking forward to holding the baby in my arms and taking care of him/her. I was actually beginning to be happy about having a baby.

My family in Alabama wasn't so supportive. My father couldn't understand why we didn't get married and said some horrible things about me and the baby. That didn't seem to matter much because throughout my life, the only time I really had interaction with him was when I was made to visit him in the summer. Through the year we spoke over the phone periodically. He later told me it hurt him less if he didn't speak to me or write. So our interaction now that I was pregnant was pretty much the same and that was fine with me.

I knew for sure that no matter what I had to do, my child would never, ever be made to feel like I've felt all my life. I always felt like my father didn't care much for me and I felt like I was a burden to Mom. Many times I convinced myself her life would be so much easier without me. She was the best mom she could've been under our extreme circumstances. I wanted to be like her. She loved her children, and I already loved mine. I was all in about this baby whether anyone else was or not!

ANGELS

There were always good people (I call them my angels) around me, mostly guys, who took it upon themselves to take care of me. Why, I'll never understand. Maybe because my father was absent or they felt sorry for me, I don't know, but they protected me in many ways. I'm sure I would be more messed up than I was had it not been for them. They loved me and accepted me for whom I was. I was safe with them in every way.

I had some wonderful friends during this time in my life as well, those who never treated me differently because I was pregnant and unmarried. They loved and accepted me, and tried to help me.

I hoped this child I was carrying would always have people to look out for him/her like I did. When I was too messed up to care for myself (or just didn't care) someone was always around to see to me. I hoped the same for my child. Even though I hadn't given God a second thought (except to think I was totally forgotten by Him) I did believe in angels, those assigned to you for your good.

My best friend and I were pregnant at the same time. As I look back writing this story, I think that was a "provision" of sorts for me. She was married and settled and often I'd listen to her talk and realize what I was thinking or feeling was actually kind of normal. That was so reassuring.

At that time, 1982, we didn't have access to much information regarding pregnancy. I don't recall hearing anything bad about pregnancy and childbirth. Everyone it seemed had their babies and lived happily ever after. How in the world would I pull that off, I wondered.

I had a general practitioner as my OB/GYN. I didn't know what to ask, what to feel so I just listened. I read the books and materials he gave me to read. I had married friends who had kids but for some reason I was too shy, too ashamed to talk to them about how I was feeling so we all just kind of went with it.

Looking back, I see all that as provision. Just to be around people who tried to help me and let me peek into their lives was how I gained what little knowledge about being a parent I got. I just didn't know if we would ever get married or really settle down to be a family.

I didn't know what it was like to be a "family." I never had one, at least back then I didn't. That's the one thing I yearned for: a real family. I wanted my baby to know security and love. I wanted him/her to have a guarantee that he or she would never be left or wonder if he or she were loved. That was my goal. I wanted this child to know that kind of love I never knew, so that's what I aimed for. I didn't know where we would lay our heads, whether his dad would be with us or not, or what would happen to us but I did know this baby was going to know real love.

WADDLING THROUGH

Waddle,
      waddle,
            waddle.
On my way to the bathroom again. I was miserable. I couldn't even see my feet anymore, let alone tie my own shoes. Of course, that wasn't really a problem because none of my shoes fit! My feet seemed to have borne the brunt of my enormous size. My normally petite size-7 foot had blossomed to a size 8½, which was normal, wasn't it, for a woman nine months' pregnant?

    I was still working, still trying to maintain my life just exactly as I felt it should be. I was determined that this baby wasn't going to change a thing, because I refused to let it. I could still go wherever I wanted and do whatever I wanted I'd just take my child with me. Nothing would change. I promised myself.

    I was still very much in control of me — the thought of which sounded ridiculous, considering my circumstances. But, it was still my life (such as it was) and I wouldn't let anything interfere with the life I had come to terms with. True, being pregnant and unmarried changed what little bit of life I had come to know.

At this point, I wondered if I should give the baby up for adoption. After all, a couple could give this child financial security, a stable home life, things I probably would never be able to give. Was I being selfish? I mean, shouldn't I do what was really BEST for the baby? I was fairly sure my best would never be good enough. I didn't even deserve to be a mother. Not only that, I had failed at everything my "prophecy" was that I would never be anything. Why would I want to pass my curse onto an innocent life? I talked to someone about adoption without anyone knowing and their advice was to "follow my heart." So I did; I would keep my baby. I knew it would be hard but at this point, perhaps selfishly, I couldn't picture my life without this child.

I never believed in abortion, even as out of control and wild as I was so that wasn't an option. I was going to be a mommy—I would just incorporate the baby in. And after all, with my decision to have the baby, what choice did I have? I mean I did this to myself. As my father had said, "you made this bed, you lay in it!" So I started preparing myself for the baby and I was actually okay with it. I would be a good mother, that much I knew. I just hoped that would be enough. My child would never be made to feel like I've felt. This baby would know love. At least I could do that. That was my only plan for motherhood: love my child regardless.

Mom and my sister continued to be wonderfully supportive and loving. My sister would pat my growing belly and talk to the baby whom she called 'Buddy'.

At least I realized I needed to do what was right for the life I was carrying. I couldn't just think about me anymore. I did my best as a mommy-to-be, got plenty of rest, took my vitamins, and I felt great. I followed instructions for a healthy pregnancy to the letter. Even though the situation was wrong, I tried to do everything right.

God must've known something absolutely major would have to happen to get me to stop my self-destructive lifestyle and my self-hatred. Little did I know how the course of my life was dramatically changing. Doing what was best for the baby was only a first step in a very long process.

"For I know the plans I have for you...declares the Lord...plans to prosper you and not harm you, plans to give you hope and a future." Jeremiah 29:11

Up until the last couple of months I had an uncomplicated pregnancy and I felt better than I had in my life. Close to the end of my pregnancy, things started changing and I realized that maybe, just maybe, I wasn't as in control of my destiny as I thought I was.

READY FOR BABY, BABY NOT READY

December 22, 1982 was my due date. Other than that, it was just another day. On that very cold day, I got up and went to work as usual. My family was preparing for Christmas, and everyone was preparing for a Christmas baby - my side of the family's first grandchild - so you can imagine, everyone was pretty excited. They were all absolutely determined that this WOULD be a Christmas baby.

This was the first time in a long time I was excited about Christmas. Holidays were horrible when I was younger. They were filled with arguments and tension about where we would spend them. Then there were the money issues. They just seemed to be more trouble than they were worth. I wondered if I would have a Christmas baby. That would be a memory, now wouldn't it?

I was at work and felt a little nauseated, went to the bathroom (again) and noticed that I had passed some blood. I called my doctor's office and went in for an exam, but everything was totally normal with no signs of an impending birth. The doctor determined that this was probably "bloody show, mucus plug" nothing abnormal. After all this was my due date, and this probably meant that labor was just around the corner. However, just to be on the safe side, and since it was so late in my pregnancy, he decided to send me for an ultrasound.

In those days, ultrasounds weren't done as frequently as they are now. They were only ordered if there were concerns. They were also done a bit differently back then than they are now. I would love to know who invented this grand idea for a woman nine months pregnant to drink gallons of water and not use the bathroom, while the whole time the baby inside of you is pressing right up against your bladder making you totally miserable. This process had to have been designed by someone who had

But Grace Prevailed

never been pregnant and certainly wasn't pregnant when they experienced one of these.

The ultrasound took approximately TWO hours! Thankfully at some point, they finally let me relieve my bladder and the ultrasound continued. Something wasn't right. I could feel it. Two technicians came and looked, rolled the wand over my very active belly, and watched for a long time. One of the on-call OB/GYN doctors came in to see the ultrasound then the radiologist was called in. I must say, I can see why - it was quite a spectacular show! The baby kicked the wand out of their hands on more than one occasion. They finally let me see the screen, and I was truly amazed! I could see the baby's face, nose, eyes, and mouth! I could also see the baby's hands and I counted five fingers on each. We could see this great detail because the baby was so large; remember, I was nine months' pregnant! The technology was not as sophisticated as it is now, but this was amazing to all of us.

After the radiologist rolled around on my belly for a while, the test was finally finished and he called my doctor. I was told to sit just outside the radiologist's office while he made the call and I could hear the conversation. The radiologist was obviously upset as he was rather loud. I heard him ask my doctor several times to "at least" get a second opinion - or to admit me for observation. After they were finished with their discussion, I spoke to my doctor on the radiologist's phone and he told me that a lot of times with a baby at this stage of pregnancy, ultrasounds were not accurate, and he believed that God was in control of childbirth.

God. In charge. Hmmm? That was a foreign concept to me and frankly it messed me up. God. In control. So this unplanned pregnancy of this unmarried young woman was God being in control. Maybe. I wasn't trying to be in control, now was I? Was this pregnancy His *plan*? Maybe someone should tell Him about whose belly this baby is in. He needs to know He may have messed up. *Hello, God? Are you there? Do you have any idea who I am? I'm the one who is supposed to be a nothing; I'm a flop, a failure. I think maybe you made a mistake. Do you hate me? Do you hate this baby you're supposedly in 'control' of? If you love this baby why did you give it to me? Yep, you've definitely made a mistake…*

The test showed the baby's heart and liver were enlarged, and there was a large amount of meconium (a baby's first bowel movement) in the gut, but my placenta was intact and everything else looked fine. The doctor believed it would be best to let nature take its course.

Now, I should tell you here that, obviously, I knew nothing. I was dumb as a rock when it came to being pregnant. And, I was very naive. I trusted my doctor implicitly. After all, he was a doctor and questioning a doctor was out of the question back then. I felt my only recourse was to do what he said and let 'nature take its course'. So, even after the radiologist told me he was very concerned and after talking to my doctor, I chose to follow his instructions, go home and wait. My doctor told me that I could still carry on with my "normal" plan for as long as I felt like it so I did, right up until the day I went into labor.

December 28, 1982 was just another day, nothing special, other than the fact that I was very pregnant and very tired. The mundane routine of getting back to normal after the Christmas holidays, exchanging unwanted gifts, getting back into the routine of work after the holidays was particularly exhausting that year. Only one thing was remarkable about that date, that year. I was pregnant, past my due date, and unusually sleepy. I talked to my bosses, and we collectively decided that since I was past due I should discontinue work, go home to rest and wait.

I had stopped on the way home and gotten fresh pasta and fresh ingredients to make some homemade spaghetti. After eating, I slept for the rest of the day. I was living with Mom who came in and checked on me several times. I just couldn't stay awake. When I finally got up, I was having some unusual discomfort and laughed telling her how funny it would be after eating all that spaghetti if I was in labor. Sure enough that's exactly what it was. And it wasn't funny!

I called my boyfriend who was spending the holiday out of town with his family and told him I was in labor. Not long after he arrived, my contractions were six minutes apart so we were off to the hospital.

We got checked into Labor and Delivery and prepared for what hopefully would be a short time before the baby was born. Hours went by. We waited. I contracted. We waited. I was sick. We waited. The hours crept by. My doctor came in and examined me and said we were still a way from delivery and decided to give me something to relax which stopped my contractions completely and I slept for several hours. When I woke up, my contractions resumed, but I was not progressing well.

So, after several more hours of unprogressive labor, he came in, checked me again and said that I hadn't dilated anymore and that it would be a while. This was somewhere around 5:00, which meant I had been in hard labor for approximately 15 hours.

Needless to say, I was absolutely exhausted. I had stopped vomiting, and I remember that I felt very strange like I had some kind of an inside program making me see and sense what was going on. But I couldn't *feel* anything. Maybe it was physical fatigue, maybe I was dehydrated and in shock - I don't know. I choose to believe that God had taken over and put me "outside of me," like I was a spectator watching all of this unfold. He did that, I believe, to help me reserve my strength for a time when I would later have to fight hard, harder than I ever had to fight in my life.

It was at that time that everything started swirling downhill –

THE ARRIVAL

My doctor decided to send me to x-ray to see if I could accommodate the birth. On the way down to x-ray, my water broke and it was green, olive green. I left a trail all the way down the hall and it was all over me. It was everywhere! I was mentally out of it, as I said above. And, even though my precious attendant, an elderly volunteer, told me that my water had broken and that she was quite concerned when she saw the color, it never crossed my mind that anything was wrong. I was just glad because I knew it wouldn't be long until the baby would be here. I was oblivious.

When I returned to my room, the doctor decided to give me Pitocin to enhance my contractions. After the Pitocin, the baby's heartbeat became irregular and the variability wasn't good, so my nurse (who was a woman I had gone to school with) checked me and asked an OB/GYN to come in and check me. She had tried to call my doctor but he wasn't there, so she grabbed one walking by.

By then, I had started running a fever and I was more mentally incoherent. As I look back while writing this, I remember feeling like a robot, that something was holding me down and I couldn't react to anything. I now believe I was in that state so I wouldn't use all of my energy coming apart. God knew I would need my energy and a clear mind, later...

My doctor was content to let my labor progress but apparently, the nurse was worried, thank God! She literally went down the hall and grabbed another OB doctor that was on the floor and told him that she couldn't get in touch with my doctor. She asked him to check me because her concerns. He came in and checked me, the baby's heart rate, and within five minutes, they were rolling me down the hall, prepping my stomach en-route for an emergency C-section. I still couldn't react. I just rolled, literally, with the flow.

THE BEGINNING...OR THE END?

Thirty years ago, they put women to sleep for C-sections, especially those of us who had an emergency situation. And fathers weren't allowed in the operating room, even under the best of circumstances. I remember going into the operating room and the anesthetist trying to talk to me. I remember the staff trying to pick me up and put me on the operating table between contractions, which was a real fiasco because the contractions (because of the Pitocin) were coming at about a minute apart. I was contracting almost constantly. In midair, they were grabbing my arms and strapping them down. They were putting more IVs in, and placing a mask over my face. Before I felt the operating table beneath me, I was out.

I woke up in the recovery room and was I ever glad about that. That meant the ordeal was over. Or was it? I awoke with the nurse pushing on my postoperative belly, which was more painful than I can describe. Unless you've experienced that firsthand, you wouldn't understand anyway. After I had some words with her (much too coarse to repeat here), I remembered our Lamaze training. The nurse practitioner told us that if we had a C-section, when we awoke in recovery to look at our arm band to see what we had. A pink armband signified a girl; blue meant a boy. I looked.

NO ARM BAND!

I sat straight up in the bed and screamed out, "Where's my arm band?" "Where's my baby?" I can close my eyes even now, 30 years later and remember the looks on the faces of the nurses. I remember two of them standing at the desk for a minute, whispering to one another, then one of them coming over there to tell me that they would call and check and see.

There was my memory again. I remembered being that 6-year-old girl looking in the mirror hearing, *"Bless her heart, she doesn't stand a chance; she'll never amount to nothin'!"* That same look is what my aunts gave each other that night. I got that same look the first time Mom came home early and found me drunk. That, "I feel so sorry for her, the poor pitiful thing" look. That's when I knew, I KNEW something was terribly wrong.

The reason I didn't have a pink or a blue arm band was that, technically, when my son was born, he was dead. He wasn't breathing. They put a tube down his throat and resuscitated him for 11 minutes. When he began breathing, he had seizures so severe that he stopped breathing, so in all actuality, when I left the operating room to go to recovery, I had no baby because no one thought he was going to live. They were fairly doubtful that I would.

The situation was grim, to say the least. Shortly after I found out that I had a boy and that he was alive (that's all they would tell me), they put a blue bracelet on my arm. After that, the baby's father and Mom came in to see me.
They told me they had seen the baby, but that's all. My son's father told me I could name him whatever I wanted to which definitely

confirmed my suspicions of something being very wrong. We had picked out a girl's name at the beginning of my pregnancy but we couldn't agree on a boy's name. When he said I could pick the name and it could be whatever I wanted, I asked him to spill it and tell me what was wrong. He told me that it was nothing to worry about and that everything was fine. I looked in their eyes and knew that they weren't telling me something but again, I was looking at them through feverish eyes, and the window that God had placed me behind.

All I could think about was that I was a mother. My baby was here! I still had the nagging, anxious feeling that something wasn't right.

After my recovery room experience, I was wheeled to the Labor and Delivery floor. Along the way, they stopped and showed me the baby. It was late, so the halls were dark and I didn't have my glasses on. They opened the curtains to what I now know was the Neonatal ICU nursery. And there he was, far across the room, so I couldn't see much (another blessing in itself). I could see that he appeared to have lots of equipment around him and on him. He was the only baby in that section. *My baby*. MY baby. The staff with me didn't say a word, and I didn't ask any questions. Strange silence. Strange everything. Even Mom was quiet. Nobody even offered to get my glasses so I could see him better. So I just played along in the moment. I still felt "outside myself," like I was an observer to even what I was feeling.

I assumed that was normal; I had no point of comparison. I didn't know how much was really wrong. I thought I was feeling the way I was because of the anesthesia and the effects of long labor. I was so tired, so elated I was finally a Mom. So scared. So happy. So sad that I couldn't hold him or see him clearly.

I remember feeling this way so many times in my life. Should I be happy? Was it wrong to be happy? I mean, after all, I wasn't married and I had a baby. Something was going on and no one would tell me what it was. Should I be sad? Mad? Hurt? What was normal? This was my "normal" now. Was that good? Bad?

I learned the next morning the baby was on a ventilator with multiple tubes stuck everywhere in his little body. He was green. He had laid in "meconium" (that first bowel movement) so long that his hands and his feet were wrinkled and green. His lips were green. He was unconscious, heavily sedated on antiseizure medications, including Dilantin and Phenobarbital. Because when he was not sedated, he was constantly seizing. Which meant his central nervous system would become paralyzed again, and he would stop breathing. This risked more brain damage. Every time they stuck him for blood work or even provided him the slightest human stimulation he had grand mal seizures. Not only that, he had no urine output and he had yet to cry. He was just a lifeless, green baby about whom everyone thought that it was just a matter of time before he died.

All I could see was a body in a huge box with lights and equipment all over it. Little did I know that they were just sustaining his life.

I had a fever, and was extremely groggy but, dumb as I was, I thought all of that was normal after just having had a baby by C-section. It never occurred to me how sick I was, that my life was in danger. Apparently the meconium the baby was laying in had caused an infection which, when he was delivered, contaminated my entire abdomen including my bladder and kidneys. Both of us were in critical condition and things could go either way. I had no idea!

The next morning, as best I can remember, Mom was there and she started telling me how sick the baby was. She had been there all night which I thought was kind of strange, but that was my mom for you. She was always there if her children were sick or things weren't right. Her whole life was devoted to her two girls, so I just thought she was doing the mom thing! I don't remember exactly what she said, but I do remember how adamant she was that I understand how sick he was which made me mad. She had a tendency to exaggerate and make things worse than what they really were. I told her I didn't believe her because if that were true, the doctor would have told me that himself.

I should explain here that the doctor that performed the emergency C-section wasn't the doctor who followed me throughout my pregnancy. My OB (we'll call him Dr. Gray) couldn't perform surgery so the doctor my nurse/friend called in to examine me actually performed the surgery. It was told to me Dr. Gray was in the operating room and when they took the baby, he ran out of the operating room.

THE TRUTH ABOUT TRUTH

About that time, Dr. Gray came in. He told me there were "complications" and that the baby was "holding his own" and he would eventually be fine. He said it was because the labor process was extremely long (23 hours) and difficult for him but he was making progress and he would see what he could do to make arrangements for me to see him. So, I was satisfied.

Not too long after that, Dr. Gray called back to my room and they had done a skull x-ray (because the baby wouldn't stop seizing) and sure enough, they had found a skull fracture and now that they knew what the problem was, everything was going to be fine, just fine.

That was the last time I heard from or saw Dr. Gray. The OB who delivered my baby assumed my care from there, and they told me a neurological specialist was called in for my son and had stayed the night with him and when he felt he could, he would come to talk to me. We later found out that he didn't have a skull fracture; it was a bleb on the x-ray. So, what was wrong? I was confused. Why would he tell me that? No one knew. No one had any answers and no one could tell me why my baby was so sick. He was in the Neonatal Intensive Care Unit and it looked like he would be there a while.

The pediatrician came in and after hearing what I was told, he was furious. He told me my baby was NOT fine, and that he was very close to death. They couldn't control the seizures. He had no urine output since he was born. He had probable pneumonia from aspirating the meconium he had apparently laid in for what appeared to be a long time since his hands, nails, and skin were green tinged. If I was in denial after he finished what he had to say, I became fully aware of the seriousness of the situation. Talk about a wake-up call. Too real, if you ask me.

Seriously? To whom does this stuff happen? This whole thing was becoming like some kind of movie you go to see after returning to your normal life. My life had never been normal. Why was I stupid enough to believe that having a baby would be normal? This is the curse, the words spoken into my life when I was a kid: *"Doesn't stand a chance...never be anything...."* I should have known better than to think otherwise. And where was this God I kept hearing about? Did HE cause this? Or was this because He had forgotten me, or I Him? I didn't know Him and seriously doubted He had anything to do with me. No. This was all my fault. This was my punishment for how I had lived. This baby was going to die and it was all my fault. That was my truth, my responsibility. My fault.

CONFIRMATION

So there I was. The girl that nothingness was prophesied over. The lost cause, it turns out, couldn't even have a baby right. Just my luck. Why did I ever expect anything other than bad could come from even this situation? Now I had messed up another person's life. Or, even worse, an innocent baby's life. Why was I even allowed to have children? Of all the women in the world that deserved babies, I wasn't one. Out of all the people I knew who had children I had never even heard of anything like this happening to any one of them. If there was ever a time that proved to me what a failure and mess-up I was, it was that moment after the doctor told me how bad things were. *Nothing…no chance...*absolutely confirmed! I was an absolute failure at everything I touched, even life.

On my second hospital day, Mom unexpectedly came by to find me walking down the hall. I kept hearing the nurses bring babies to the other new moms but no one brought my baby to me, so I decided that I was going to go to him. Never mind that they had legitimate reasons for that: I had a rampant infection with a very high fever and the baby, of course, was very sick. Obviously, I still wasn't thinking rationally. Mom yelled at me from the end of the corridor. I couldn't understand what all the fuss was about. I just wanted to see my baby! I had a temperature of 103, I couldn't keep any food down, but I thought that it was all a normal process after a C-section. How was I supposed to know? I'd never had a baby before and no one told me any differently!

After I got back into bed (I never made it to see my son) she told me that a neonatal specialist was being called in to see the baby and she would have my doctor come and talk to me. The baby's pediatrician came in and he was still pretty upset. He told me that my baby was NOT all right and he was NOT going to be all right, and if anybody indicated otherwise, they were "wearing rose-colored glasses." He told me the baby was very, very sick and very close to death. And, until the neurologist and another specialist saw him, he couldn't tell me anything other than that. He just wanted me to understand that the situation was very serious.

JUST A PEEK OF REALITY

I think it was about that time that reality began to set in. I knew I had to snap out of this fog I was in before it was too late. I had to get to my baby. Finally they agreed to take me down in a wheelchair so that I could see for myself - after all, it was my son's second day of life and I hadn't really gotten to see him yet.

To my surprise and disappointment, when we got to the nursery, they would only let me see him through the glass. I couldn't go in, and I couldn't touch him. I could only look and long to hold him. That moment is a significant one in my memory, and I don't think I will ever forget it. I looked over at his incubator, that huge box of a thing with all the lights, and I was overcome with grief. There he was, so lifeless not moving at all. He was on a ventilator with tubes and things everywhere. He didn't even have a diaper on. His hands, fingernails, feet and toenails were green.

One of the nurses (whom I also had gone to school with) came out to talk to me and right there, in that hallway, with my face pressed up against that Newborn Intensive Care Nursery window, the full weight of the situation began to invade my mind and my heart. I was coming out of it. I finally was beginning to understand that there was a very serious, very scary thing, going on here.

I looked at that lifeless little baby and my heart broke. He didn't move. I couldn't even see his chest move with the sound of the respirator. No twitch, no stretch, nothing. He never opened his eyes the entire time I was there. He was just lying there like a doll that someone had forgotten to dress. I thought, *"That can't be my baby….that can't be my baby….that can't be my baby. This must be a dream!"*

As per my norm when I found myself in a threatening situation or something hurt me, I began to feel rage. I was so mad and so hurt. I wanted them to be wrong so badly. I wanted this to be an overdramatized dream, but I knew in my heart they were right. Looking at him told me they were right. This definitely wasn't a dream.

Mom wheeled me to my room. When I returned down the hall, I had been changed to a private room. To compound our situation, I finally realized that I really was very sick. When they did my C-section, all that meconium (the baby's first bowel movement) seeped into the rest of my abdominal cavity because of a uterine tear. It had apparently been leaking for some time because this green stuff was oozing from my abdominal incision. My urine was green. And the normal, bloody drainage that occurs after childbirth was sometimes tinged green. Nasty, to say the least. I had a major infection going on and had become septic, which meant the infection had gone into my blood stream.

My situation was grim enough to justify a private room and a critical condition status. So, my family began their around-the-clock vigil just in case I died, the baby died, or we both died. Family members poured in and they consumed my room and the hallway. They also didn't want to expose any of the other new mothers to my infectious germs I was apparently carrying.

Some of my friends were told they couldn't see me because I was critical. I found out later another reason they moved me to a private room was that they didn't want me to see the other new moms getting to hold and feed their new babies because, in all likelihood, I would never have that privilege.

FAMILY PLAYS FAMILY

That same day, Mom called Dad who talked to the neonatologist about my son's condition. The doctor told him if he wanted to see his grandson (and me) alive, he needed to come, and the sooner he could get here, the better. So Dad, his wife, and my sister drove in from Alabama to see us not knowing whether they would make it in time.

When they arrived, I remember I was asleep and woke up to him kissing me on the forehead and taking my hand in his. As I look back on that time, I think that I must've been as really close to death as everyone said I was. I remember I would go to sleep and, every time I dreamed, I was caught in a dark tunnel. The voices of the people I loved would fade...fade...fade. And I would start spinning and whirling down. Things would get brighter. I would almost be at the end of the tunnel then I would wake up gasping for air.

Such was the case when I felt my father kiss my forehead. I knew when I saw his face that he was worried. They had driven for a long time to get there. Besides that, I could count on one hand the times he came to visit my whole life so for them to be there was another indication that the situation was very, very grim.

He found all the doctors and talked to them about me and the baby. He, being a pharmacist, and my mother, a nurse, probably understood how dismal the situation was, definitely better than I would allow myself to, so they rarely left my side and if they weren't in my room, they were standing there, helplessly looking in that nursery window when the drapes were opened. Most of the time, though, the drapes were drawn, and that wasn't a good sign. If the drapes were drawn, that meant they were working on one of the babies, and the longer the curtain stayed shut the more serious the situation was. The drapes on the ICU nursery were shut more often than opened.

-Photo Album-

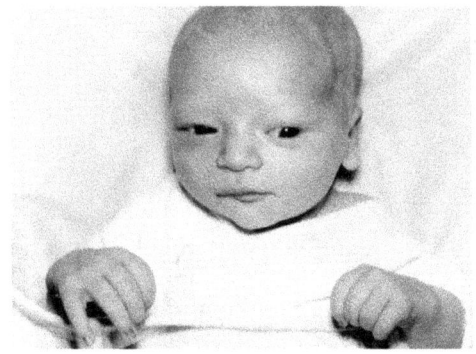

"Green" Baby

Barbara McGreger

Home from the Hospital

Nine Months Old

But Grace Prevailed

First Camping Trip

Two Years Old

Camping, Three Years Old

But Grace Prevailed

Halloween, Four Years Old

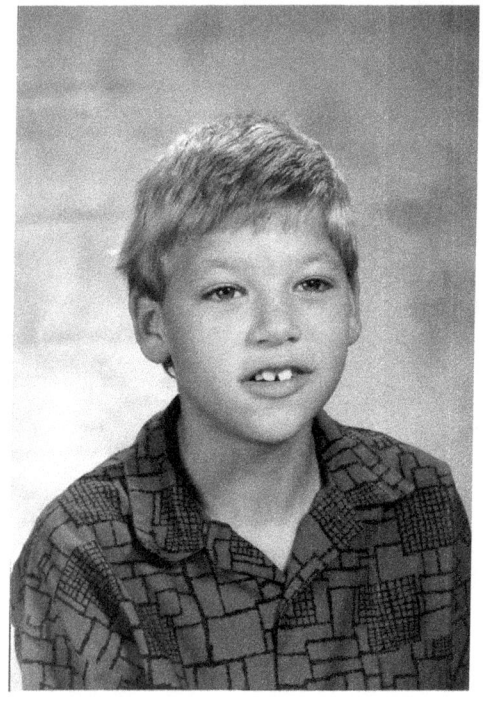

Nine Years Old

But Grace Prevailed

On Stage with Randy Owen

Karate Class

Barbara McGreger

Senior Portrait, Age 19

Matt

CONFRONTATION OF TRUTH

Late the afternoon of the third day, the neonatologist who had been called in when my son was born came in to see us. He asked everyone to leave the room so he could talk to me and the baby's father alone. My heart sank. This couldn't be good. Otherwise, he would want everyone to hear. Mom and my sister were there; Dad and his wife had gone to their hotel to clean up and to rest a bit.

The doctor pulled a chair up to my bedside. He looked almost as bad as I did. His eyes were bloodshot. He had a beard growing. He looked just awful. Turns out he had been with my son for a 48-hour stretch, rarely leaving his side.

The doctor solemnly explained that he had done everything he could think to do and the baby was showing no improvement. As a matter of fact, he had taken a turn for the worse. There was still no urine output, and every time they weaned him from the medication with the slightest touch, he would begin seizing. At that point, he said that he felt obligated to discuss our options with us, that we may want to consider taking him off the ventilator and "let him go." Literally every time the little fellow was touched or stimulated in any way, he would start having seizures so severe that he would have to be resuscitated.

He told us there was one more thing, the *last* thing he wanted to try before we should make those decisions. He said it was an extremely long shot, but the only shot we had left. He felt that it just may turn the baby around and he wanted us to consider it.

He explained that the "mother-baby bonding process" sometimes awakened the baby's capacity and will to keep fighting. He said he had seen situations when just the touch and the voice of the mother would be enough to give the baby incentive to turn around and the will to live. He told us that it was an extreme longshot, but it was our last resort. He said it couldn't hurt. He wanted me and the baby's dad to go in and finally be with our son. This was the only thing he knew to do because everything else had been done and that if this didn't work we needed to realistically prepare for "letting him go."

There was another complication to my being able to see my baby. Because of my still very high fever, they were going to have to remove all the other babies, (four as best I can recall) out of that section of the ICU nursery so as not to expose them to anything, and put up partitions between our son and another baby girl who was too critical to move, and then they would come and get me to see my son.

My time had come. Finally, finally, finally, I was going to get to hold my baby.

THE FIRST (AND MAYBE LAST) ENCOUNTER

Needless to say, I was excited and terrified at the same time. What if he didn't respond? What if he died in my arms? What if I died before I got to hold him? I had no idea; no idea what was about to happen. There were so many terrifying possibilities to prepare for in such a short time.

What if he hated me? What if he had no recognition of me at all? After all, this was my fault. I was responsible for him being in the shape he was in because I had him. The lost cause had wrongly become his mom. So that put it all on me, didn't it? What if he hated me because he had become part of my curse?

He still had no urine output and was on extremely high doses of medications to control his seizures. Regardless, I was so excited. Regardless of what had happened, I would finally get to touch him and to tell him how sorry I was. I remember craving, crying and grieving just to touch him. Part of me was missing and it was finally time to put us back together.

Can you imagine, you that are mothers reading this? Can you imagine giving birth to a baby and waiting three long, agonizing days before getting to hold your newborn? That little life that grew inside you, and kicked and squirmed all those months? And now you do not have access to him? To make it worse, he was sick. He needed his Mommy and his Mommy needed him. Those days were agonizing, terrifying, confusing and infuriating. But, finally, the time had come for me to reintroduce myself to my son.

My family was happy for me and sad at the same time. None of us knew what to expect or what would happen. It may be that I wouldn't even get to hold him. My heart was going to beat out of my chest. I was scared to death, but so excited. Fearful yet thrilled. Would this be a good-bye? I tried to put those thoughts aside and just be glad I was finally getting to at least touch him. I convinced myself that no matter what, I'd relish my minutes with him. I knew this would be a significant moment in my life and it would make me an official Mom.

Still I couldn't help but feel guilty that he got stuck with me. I was so scared that I could somehow mess this encounter up. What if I got sick? What if I hurt him? I didn't tell anyone what I was feeling as usual. I kept all the self-mutilation and doubt to myself like it was a prized possession.

It was really happening! The wheelchair lady came in as well as two other nurses to help with the IV's (too many for just one attendant) and we were on our way down that hall toward my prize. The hall seemed to go on forever. I wanted to say, *"Okay, girls, can we go faster?"* When we got to the nursery, a nurse came out and told us we would have to 'gown up' before we could go near him. We had to sterilize our hands and put on gowns, which seemed to take forever. I was so excited and so scared for so many reasons. I was sweating and I was sure my heart was going to jump from my chest! I looked out the window from *inside* the nursery this time. And there was my whole family standing there. Teary-eyed and with great anticipation, they were waiting for the moment that I would get to hold my son. They were holding their breaths that this was really going to happen.

Finally, the unit supervisor in attendance with two doctors showed me all the stuff he was plugged up to and what each was for. Because he was heavily sedated, he was not on the ventilator at that time. He had an oxygen hood over him (it looked like the thing on a hair dryer that you put your head under at the beauty shop) with a tube that blew oxygen into his nose and mouth while in the tent-like thing he was in. They put two rocking chairs by his incubator, then they lifted that tiny green-tinged, lifeless baby up, turned around and headed toward me, his Mommy.

I couldn't wait to get my hands on him. How would he know I was even there I mean, would he? He was so lifeless. They placed him in my arms and I snuggled him up. I don't think anything in my entire life felt so good and so right to me as holding him in my arms that first time. I felt complete, like being that baby's mom was exactly what I was supposed to do. I think it was the first time I felt a sense of purpose. I felt better than I had in days. During that first moment he was in my arms, I knew I was meant to be his mother…his *mommy*.

Despite all my ugliness, feelings of failure, and the guilt of what was happening to him, I have never felt more complete, more *right*. He was mine. Whether or not he ever woke up, whether or not he lived from these precious moments on, he was mine. It was real and I wanted to make sure he knew who had their arms around him. He was going to hear me. He was going to feel me. He was going to know that I was there, that his mommy was there. I wanted him to know how much I loved him. I said, "Hey, Buddy (what I called him when I was pregnant) it's Mommy. Hey, baby boy, it's Mommy." As soon as I got the words out of my mouth, that little pitiful looking baby…

Opened…his…eyes…and looked up at me! He recognized my voice! He opened his eyes! He opened his eyes! HE OPENED HIS EYES! Not for long, but he opened his eyes and he looked right at me as if to say, "Oooh, *there* you are!" I started crying. His dad gasped then started laughing. What an amazing moment. He hadn't been conscious in two days. He was heavily sedated but, when I spoke to him, he opened those eyes. I heard cheers from the other side of the nursery window. My family was rejoicing. I'm crying again as I write this and remember this precious moment, one of the most poignant of my life to this day.

I caught a glimpse of God that night. I saw something greater than me working in that nursery that I'll never forget. The nurses and the doctor had tears streaming down their faces.
I heard squeals of joy from the other side of the glass. Because they had their faces pressed up against the glass, everyone saw what had happened. He, for real and for the first time since he was born, opened his eyes! He looked right up at me, just for a couple of seconds and then closed them.

I held him for a few minutes. I put my hand over his chest to feel his heart beating, and it was racing. Before that they told me his heart rate had been very slow. One of his little, green-tinged hands moved a little bit, just a tiny little bit.

Something inside me came alive. And I knew that moment had changed the atmosphere in the nursery. I could literally *feel,* not only see, that this was a significant moment in our lives, one that, as long as I live, I will never ever forget. This was the game-changer; the sign so many had prayed for and I had hoped for. I knew when I got pregnant everything about my life would change but I didn't get that then but I surely did when he was in my arms.

Needless to say, I was so elated, I don't even remember being wheeled back to my room – all I could think about was, *"He opened his eyes!"*

The next thing I remember was seeing family members I hadn't seen in a long time. They had all been summoned for a death vigil, coming to say goodbye to me and to see the baby they were told would never leave the hospital. My Aunts (the same ones who told me I would never be anything and didn't stand a chance) told me I was going to be fine; I could have other babies. They made me so mad. They had already given up on him but I refused to. "I DON'T WANT ANOTHER BABY! I WANT HIM!" I know they meant well and were trying to prepare me. In my mind, he was being written off just like I had always been and I just wasn't going to let that happen. I refused to believe he was going to die.

Finally everyone cleared out and I was given a sleeping pill. I was still running a high fever and physically felt horrible but I couldn't stop thinking about holding my baby for the first time. I remember getting sleepy though, and drifting off to sleep feeling like a real mom and being more content than I had ever been, even knowing I may never get to hold him again. I got to hold him once and after all we had been through, for now, that was more than enough.

THE CHANGE

If you've ever been in the hospital, you know it's no place to rest. The nurses woke me up to take my vital signs and I remember my sheets were wet, like someone had spilled something on me, or bathed me while I was asleep. My fever had broken! It was 100.2, the first time in three days that it had been below 103. Just as my sheets had gotten changed and I had been cleaned up and gotten into a fresh hospital gown, the neurologist came in.

Oh no, I remember thinking. We've lost him. I got a glimpse of his face and saw he was smiling which was the first time I'd seen him do that. He had tears in his eyes. He grabbed my hand and told me the baby's body temperature had risen to 97.4! His body temperature was extremely low never higher than 96.9, from the time of birth until now. Not only that, but for the first time since he was born, he had passed urine. The doctor said that it must have been the bonding. He just needed his mommy and his mommy surely needed him.

"But may the God of all grace, who called us to His eternal glory by Christ Jesus, after you have suffered a while, perfect, establish, strengthen, and settle you"...1st Peter 5:10

That precious moment when I held that baby in my arms, when we held each other, our lives began. His, literally, but I knew he wasn't out of the woods yet. However, I knew in my heart that we were both well on our way to healing. For the first time since he had been born, I had *hope*. Not a bunch of hope, not a great strength in my hope, just a little taste of hope. Still, it was the first hope I'd had since I awoke from surgery and didn't find a pink or blue armband on my arm. Hope. I didn't know it then, but a whole bunch of people had been praying for us. I had no idea who God was, but I'm convinced (now) He surely knew me and without question, knew that little baby. I picture uncountable angels hovering over the nursery when I think about it now. I surely didn't deserve God's grace (or anything else) but that baby did. He was innocent and had done nothing wrong. I had done everything wrong and surely deserved everything I was getting.

Within an hour of our first "encounter" my fever started trending down and his body temperature started trending up. Signs of life began to appear. In those moments, I had my first introduction to the power of something (or someone) much bigger than the doctors, the bonding process or what had been spoken over me all those years ago and I knew it.

NOW WHAT?

The next morning, the fourth post baby day, began with the nurses coming in to change my sheets again – soaking wet from sweating out the fever. My temperature was now barely 99 and the baby's temperature was normal. Although still seizing, his seizures weren't as severe as they were less than 24 hours ago when he stopped breathing now, it was only for seconds instead of minutes. So, although still dismal, things were looking up.

The nurses came in with another surprise. They told me I may get to feed my baby sometime today! He was four days old and this would be my first opportunity to feed him, which I did. It seemed from there that things steadily progressed.

Two weeks later, we were both released from the hospital. I got to go home a day before he did, which gave us time to get baby formula, get my thoughts together, and spend the night sleeping in my bed. I didn't like leaving him, not at all but everybody made it sound like a good idea, so I went along with it. I called and visited him while he was still in the hospital. I couldn't help but think about as I left the hospital, how odd and unnatural it was for a mother of a newborn to be leaving without her baby. Frozen in my mind was the fact that it was very possible that I could have been leaving without a baby at all.

The morning I went to get him, I walked into the nursery – and he was crying. That was the first time I had heard him cry, he was so sedated to control the seizures that he barely made a sound. When he was awake, he would wiggle and sometimes nurse, but he hardly ever made a sound. The neurologist, the one caring for him, was in the nursery preparing him for discharge. He came over to me and hugged me and with tears in his eyes said, "I really never thought I'd see this one go home." The nurses let me finish his bath and dress him, and off we went to our new lives!

BEGINNINGS

I found out quickly the mommy thing was exhausting. He slept in spurts, ate a lot and, as the days went by with no seizures, we developed our own routine, our "normal." He seemed like a happy baby so I convinced myself he was going to be fine. We had a rough start but the troubles were over and we'd all live happily ever after.

One of my best friends had a baby a few days before I did, and it looked to me like our life with a child was like theirs. So I thought we were settling in nicely.

After an extended maternity time I tried to go back to work and put the baby in daycare which didn't work too well. He kept getting sick and frankly people seemed to be a little scared of him after they heard about the possibility of seizures, the medication list and nobody wanted to be liable. They would call me at the first sign of illness so I quit my job and stayed at home with him. I tried to go to school but that didn't work either. The baby stayed sick.

My not being able to work created more money problems, which compounded an already stressful situation. The baby's dad (at that point, now my husband) was in school trying to finish his degree, a sick baby, a stay-at-home wife. You get the picture. I don't think either of us wanted to be married. I think we were trying our best to do the "right thing" by our child. We tried to settle in but we both had issues. I wasn't happy that he seemed to have more freedom to come and go than I did. Our intense start was a breeding ground for discontentment and anger and there was a lot of that. I have to say, too, my husband was neglected. I didn't know how to be a decent woman and I knew nothing about being a wife, much less a mother of a sick child so I spent all my time and energy tending to the baby and not seeing to my husband.

We endured, surviving as best we could under the circumstances. My son stopped having seizures, so when he was six months old under the advice of his doctor, we weaned him off his medication. He said it was quite possible he wouldn't have any more seizures. He was developmentally delayed, however, but we could work on strengthening his muscles with exercises and stimulating him. I really thought the worst was over. At that point, I thought we may possibly have a shot of "happily ever after," a normal life. He ordered a CT scan of the brain. He was sure everything would be okay, but he wanted it just for completion's sake. They told us they'd call when the results were in.

NORMAL ISN'T HERE

The CT scan was another jolt to say the least. We physically saw the reality of my son's trauma suffered at birth and it shook the very foundation of my world. At the same time, my mother was in the hospital, and my grandfather died. The brain scan showed that there was damage to 80% of his brain. Yes, you read that correctly, 8-0 percent. The doctor called and told me we needed to come in to discuss our "options," and decide where to go from here.

I was numb. The percentage of the damage meant nothing to me because on the outside, he appeared totally "normal" So I thought this visit would be a normal six month baby visit. I can close my eyes 30 years later and see that doctor's face. I can feel the feelings I had when I was sitting in that office; I felt like we were in a vacuum and the room was spinning around and coming into me. He matter-of-factly told me the damage was so substantial that *IF* he lived to be a year old, he would probably never walk or talk. He told me to consider institutionalizing my son that a child "like him" would be better served in a facility designed to care for children with severe brain damage, and it certainly would be better for me. He told me it would be virtually impossible to care for him at home, IF he lived. He told me to stop taking him to the hospital when he had seizures, because there was really nothing they could do but sustain life, and a more merciful approach would be to let him die. He also told me that, if I decided to keep him at home, he would have to be a priority. He wasn't my mother's child, or the daycare's child – he was *my* child and *my* responsibility. If something happened and he died, at least I could have peace knowing that I did all I could do and that after all, I could have other children.

Enough! I stopped him after he said that, gathered up our things and told him that if it was the last thing I would do, I would prove him wrong! He was wrong, and I would show him he was wrong! We got in the car, and I remember just staring at that sweet little baby, with such beautiful eyes and a beautiful smile and thought the doctor had lost his mind. I told his father about the visit and he made me promise not to tell anyone how bad it was, so I didn't.

I carried all this around inside of me, and dealt with it totally alone. He couldn't face it and didn't want to talk about it. So from that point on I have never felt more alone. There I was. Stuck…trapped…it was hopeless. I had been written off and now my baby was written off. Why should I expect anything less?

I was so mad, so hurt. I think some kind of mother's instinct kicked in because at that moment I was determined my son wouldn't be made to feel the way I had felt my whole life. At that point, I really didn't know anything for sure. My goal was that **I** would prove everyone wrong. I would show them. He wasn't a lost cause! He was worth the chance for as normal a life as possible and I was going to see that he got it!

MY NEW NORMAL

Time went on and things in every corner of my life were deteriorating. My husband grew angrier and angrier – after all this was my fault. He had a little over a year of college. And he, regardless of what happened, was going to finish. If I had undergone an abortion like he wanted me to, then nobody would be suffering right now. What was he yelling about? He was at school and work and when he wasn't there, he was with his friends. My life was altered here – not his! I was the one that couldn't work, couldn't get together with my friends, and couldn't have a "normal life." I was the one making all the sacrifices, providing all the care for the baby. Life as I once knew it was gone. My plan for nothing to change, because I had a baby, was laughable. *Everything* changed.

I was miserable, scared, frustrated, and mad. I was becoming everything I never wanted to be. If it hadn't been for my determination to prove everyone wrong about my son, I would have easily given up. I didn't want this life. I wanted my child, but nothing else. Before him I didn't have any incentive to "be good" or anyone to really care for. I wanted to do right by him and I did my best.

I was guilt stricken with his diagnosis and about everything else: my marriage wasn't working because I was such a lousy person; my baby was sick because I was such a lousy person, and deserved exactly what I had gotten. Everything was totally my fault. The failure has failed yet again. The only thing good in my life was this baby.

CHOICES, LIFE OR DEATH

My mother was a nurse at the local hospital. Since we had no insurance, she talked to an occupational therapist who came to our house and showed me exercises to do with the baby. He told me to constantly stimulate him with music, reading to him, talking to him, so the challenge began. I did all those things. This baby became my focus, my project – my reason for getting up in the morning. Had I not had him in my life, I would have killed myself.

We had a distinct moment regarding life and death. We went camping with a group of our close friends and we took the baby with us. He loved being outdoors, and loved the water. We set up his playpen right next to a creek which mesmerized him. We all had a good time and our friends loved having the baby camping with us. When the baby was with us, I would wait until he was asleep to start drinking with the rest of our friends.

We all settled in for the night. I lay down with the baby and fell asleep. I heard voices outside at the campfire, a conversation I obviously wasn't supposed to hear. I saw some things that, once again, showed me how hopeless my situation was: the marriage, the sick baby, all of it. I came back to the tent and tried to sleep but couldn't so I gathered our things (my husband hadn't come back to our tent yet) and I left with the baby right at sunrise.

We were driving down a curvy road and I pulled off at a beautiful spot. I was crying so hard I couldn't see, and thought it best to stop. The baby was asleep in his car seat so I got out of the car and looked at where we were. It was a beautiful spot in Elizabethton, TN, where there was a very steep drop-off. I associated that with our lives. I thought it probably would be better had neither of us lived through the birth ordeal. Maybe it would be better to die. In those moments, I couldn't see that anything was worth going on. I was hopeless, really hopeless. I made my decision. Nobody wanted us anyway. This baby was going to grow up with a host of who-knows-what problems and he would just suffer. I would suffer. We would all suffer, and it was all my fault anyway.

So, if it was all my fault, I could fix it. I could end his suffering and my lifelong suffering right then and there. That's exactly what I decided to do. I sat there for a long time thinking all this through and had made up my mind. I threw the bottle of Rum I had almost finished the night before out of the car making sure it broke so alcohol couldn't be blamed. The baby was asleep so he wouldn't suffer. I had made up my mind to go back down the mountain, make it look as if I had missed the sharp curve in the road, and kill us both. Done.

I went back down the mountain, turned around and sped up. I was maybe 20 feet from the point at which I would veer off and something amazing happened. That little sweet boy woke up and touched my arm. I slowed down and looked over at him. He was smiling the sweetest smile. He was so beautiful. He kept rubbing my arm as if to say, "Mom, it's ok.

We're ok." I pulled over again, in the same spot, got him out of his seat, held him and cried.

What was it about this child, as dire as things were, that I saw hope and love in him? His smile and touch changed everything. He saved our lives in that moment.

GIVING HIM UP

These episodes of seizures/illnesses were frequent. Every EEG he had showed constant seizure activity. We had no money, I couldn't keep a job because the baby was so sick and everyone was afraid of him. My husband was in school. We had no choice but to move in with his parents. They were wonderful people who tried to help us in any way they could.

When Matt was around nine months old, I had to take him to an adjoining town for his monthly blood work through March of Dimes. I saw a little sign on a nurse's desk that quoted that familiar saying, *"God, grant me the serenity to accept the things that I cannot change and the ability to know the difference."* It was like reading that saying for the first time. Every word penetrated me. I read it over and over again. "GOD?" Who was that anyway? Surely he had nothing to do with me, with my baby or we wouldn't be in the predicament we were in. The baby certainly wouldn't be so sick. I mean, didn't He love babies? I was sure He didn't know I was alive. And any attempt to love me, know me, or care about me was thwarted a long time ago just because of whom I was. I ruined any possibility of God having anything to do with me a long time ago. But, maybe there was still some kind of chance he would help my son. Hmmm? Maybe he wouldn't hold his mother against him. I thought it was worth a shot to at least ask Him. I had nothing more to lose.

I looked at that beautiful child who was asleep in his "punkin" seat. He was gorgeous. I so wanted to help him but it was so obvious that I couldn't do anything for him. I couldn't give him what he needed. If God was who I had heard He was; if He was, in fact, REAL, maybe if I asked Him, maybe if I really GAVE my son to him, maybe he would overlook who I was and touch him. I thought it was worth a shot.

I grabbed the punkin seat, got on my knees right there in that waiting room and held the seat up to the ceiling. I said, *"Okay. Okay, God. I know I have never talked to you. Well, not in a long time. Once, when I was 13, at a church event. So please try to look over who's talking to you, okay?*

Please just look at my baby. Please just look at my baby. Please just see him and don't look at me because I know you'll turn away if you see me. Please help my son. Just let him live. He needs your help. He needs a miracle. Everyone has pretty much given up on him. If you are who you say you are, give me what this sign says. I get it. I can't do anything for this child but love him and it's not enough. My love won't help him, and it won't stop the seizures. It won't help him be 'normal.' I'm giving him to you. I'm accepting what I can't change and I'm asking you to help him. He's yours and I mean it. He's yours. Just let him live."

Something happened inside me that day – I felt part of the burden had been taken off me – I didn't have to carry it alone anymore. I put *the baby* in God's hands, but I didn't put *myself* in God's hands. I relinquished control of my son's life but not my own. Actually, I wasn't thinking about me at all. I wanted God to take care of my son. Still, I had a feeling of relief that I wasn't carrying this all by myself anymore.

"Be anxious for nothing but in everything by prayer and supplication, with thanksgiving, let your requests be made known to God; and the peace of God, which surpasses all understanding, will guard your hearts and minds through Christ Jesus." Philippians 4:6, 7

GOD, DID YOU HEAR ME?

Things moved along for a couple of months. Matt was now off all medications and seemed to be doing well. It was December. He was almost one. He wasn't walking, barely crawling but he was a happy baby. There was rarely a night that passed that I didn't go into his room and lay my hand on his chest to be sure he was still breathing. He had not had a seizure since birth so maybe the doctors had been wrong and things weren't quite as bad as they said they were. He was slightly behind other babies his age with muscle tone and strength, sitting up, crawling, etc., but he seemed to be doing well. I had found a job and had him in daycare.

I came home from work one day late in December, right before Christmas, and was holding him, giving him a bottle. He stopped sucking, his lips turned blue, his eyes got really red, and his eyebrows started twitching – Seizure! We ran down and got into the car to go to the hospital. He wasn't breathing, he wasn't responding and he was blue. We got to the hospital and I handed him over the counter to the receptionist, telling her that he was having a tonic/clonic seizure. They took him back and made us do the paperwork before we could go back. When we got the paperwork done, they still wouldn't let us go back. They had called a "code blue" for him which meant that he still wasn't breathing. They took us to that "room" that all hospitals have when family comes in with a member whose is in real danger, so we could be alone. I suddenly realized that I had his pacifier – I found a nurse and gave it to her and she promised that when he was responsive she would give it to him and come get us.

It seemed like an eternity, waiting in that little somber room. I was so scared – I thought, "Well apparently the doc was right and I was wrong. It's taking too long. They haven't come to get us because he is dead." About that time, a nurse came in and told us they had to resuscitate him twice and asked me a bunch of questions. Then, finally, she took us to see our baby.

He was laying on that stretcher, with stuff all over him and in him again, a flashback to when he was born. He saw me and smiled, then started seizing again. We spent two days that time in the ICU. I felt any hopes I had of things being any different from they had been the first year dwindle and slip away.

Trapped, stuck, hopeless.

I obviously didn't talk to God properly. That's it! Either that, or He didn't hear me. If an all-knowing, all-powerful God refused to answer my prayer then this whole deal was completely hopeless. We were sunk, doomed forever. I could picture Matt growing up and learning the truth about his mother and blaming me for everything and he had every right to. I felt his life was cursed, and he was being punished because of whom his mother was.

I had no hope of anything ever getting any better. This was going to be my life. A few days, maybe months of normalcy then BOOM, our ugly reality invaded. What made it worse is that I really believed this child suffered simply because he was mine. Had he been born to someone else, he wouldn't have these issues. I really believed that. I felt so responsible, incredibly guilty and I was so mad. This baby deserved so much better than the life he was handed. Is it possible to love your child so much and be so regretful he was born to you? That's how I felt. I didn't deserve such a gift and he didn't deserve to be my gift. Don't children deserve the best people for parents so they can have a decent shot at life?

I felt the strange sensation of family history repeating itself with one exception: even my parents were better than this baby's parents. Maybe I should have driven over that cliff?

The week after his birthday, he had ear tubes put in. And, after that, things seemed to become a little bit better. He had chronic ear infections which prompted the fevers, etc., which triggered seizures. No one wanted to do surgery because he was such a high risk for complications with anesthesia.

He walked at 13 months, an accomplishment I thought I would never see. He was jabbering and trying to talk so I was grateful. After all, remember, we were told that IF he lived he would never do either of those. I was satisfied with his progress and actually thought this was as good as it would get.

LIFE GOES ON

When Matt was two, we divorced. The situation had definitely taken its toll. There were no books to read about surviving what we had been through. I was a horrible wife and not a much better person, so I assumed all the responsibility for my failed marriage.

So let's review: a failed and broken childhood, a horrible daughter, couldn't have a baby right and now a failed marriage. I had such low self-esteem and felt worthless. My son was having difficulty handling his dad not being with us. We all tried to make the best out of a horrible situation, but it was just that - horrible. It seemed my son was regressing. He lost weight and, again, stayed sick all the time. I now had to go to work. I had to have a job to support us. I just thought that life was hard before; now, it became much harder and much more complicated.

Matt continued to have seizures off and on until he was three, at which time a relative told me about a specialist in Winston-Salem, North Carolina he wanted us to go and see so he called and got us in. We went to Bowman-Gray University for a week for some intense testing. That was when we got the diagnosis of cerebral palsy. Again, I felt myself going into my protective shell watching all of this unfolding, but not *feeling* it. It seemed like every time I got my feet on the ground, another office visit and another doctor would come knock me off my feet. This happened again and again and again. His head circumference had not changed since birth which meant that his brain wasn't growing. He was blind in one eye and had a speech impediment – on and on and on. It all just infuriated me! I felt rage and hate, just for life in general, just boiling inside of me. I hated everything and everybody. I hated and resented my life, my son's problems, and there wasn't anything I could do about any of it: stuck, alone, trapped, hopeless.

When he had his first MRI, it showed so much damage to the brain, the white matter couldn't be distinguished from the gray matter. The damage was extensive. The doctor said it was "miraculous" he was doing as well as he was. He was baffled and on a couple of occasions, he would bring interns in and do "show and tell" with Matt as he was one of his most extreme cases of extensive brain damage. He was just a "case," a phenomenon to them but my baby to me.

Whom does this stuff happen to? I felt like I was trapped in a movie. How could this possibly be real? What were we to do? How would this story end? Was he going to die? Where was all of this going? Nobody could give me any answers. Our lives were literally one day at a time and when that day was over, I learned to be grateful (and amazed) that we had lived through it. The smallest tasks were huge milestones, every one of them.

This child was the highlight of my life. He was my incentive to at least try to have a decent life. He deserved so much better than what I had been able to give him, so I was wrought with guilt a lot. He deserved the best medical care, the best of everything that I couldn't give him. He always seemed happy and content. His smile brightened a room. I would take him places, and wherever we were, people were drawn to him. He seemed to bring out the best in everyone he had contact with. There was something special about him. People automatically fell in love with him. His beautiful eyes and smile made everyone feel better. He changed our world into a much brighter, much more tolerable place.

Lots of family and friends, though, were afraid of him. People don't know what to do with people with disabilities. All they could think about was what if something happened to him if I was responsible for him and I understood that. Mom and my sister kept him some, and his dad's family some. Most of the time, though, it was just he and I. He did see his father, and we did attempt to work things out a couple of times, but too much damage had been done so we finally divorced.

I resumed old habits after the divorce. When Matt would go to his Dad's, I was out having a good time. I never drank when he was in my care.

I remember every milestone in that child's life. I watched him work tirelessly after I'd pick him up from daycare to teach himself how to dribble a basketball, tie his shoes, ride a bike, skate and swim (amongst other things). Each time he would set out to learn something, he worked on it almost obsessively until he mastered it. I watched him with wonder. Where did that determination come from? With each accomplishment, I would be so thankful. Because, after all, he was never supposed to have accomplished any of them.

All I asked for was that he live. I never expected him to be such a delightful child, and surely never thought I'd get to see him do all the things "normal" kids do.

"MONSIE"

As Matt grew up, he decided he needed a buddy so he created one. His name was "Monsie," an invisible friend. Monsie was quite mischievous. Every time Matt would do something he wasn't supposed to do or not do what he was told it was always Monsie's fault.

One time my sister took Matt shopping. Later when I met them there, she told me Matt had been going in and out of racks of clothes and running all over the store. When she finally caught him, his explanation for his behavior was simple! "Honey, (what Matt called her) that wasn't me, that was Monsie. I try to fowwow him to make him be good but he din't yisten to me. I try to catch him. All dat is Monsie's fault. I a good boy."

I loved Monsie. He represented a glimpse of normal to me. After all, if Matt was that creative with that kind of imagination, to me that was a wonderful thing.

One day, when he was around seven, I noticed Matt hadn't mentioned Monsie so I asked him about him. He said, "I'm grown up a little. I don't need him anymore, so I let him go. I was ready."

I cried when we lost Monsie and I'll never forget him. He was strange comfort to me. I had an invisible friend I vaguely remember. Of course, I never told Matt that. Maybe I should have.

GROWING INTO OUR "NORMAL"

We moved back to Tennessee to be with my family so they could help me, but Matt stayed sick. After about a year of that, we moved back to Alabama. He was now five, and in kindergarten. I enrolled him in school, and everyone loved him. He was originally placed in the room with the severely mentally and physically disabled children. One of his teachers came to me and told me it was imperative that we get him in a regular classroom, perhaps with an aide. Because, if he wasn't moved, he would "take on" more handicapped characteristics than he actually had. In other words, he would become what his environment taught him to be. She saw potential in him that I don't think anyone else could see, and I thank God for her.

After almost a year of fighting the system, he would repeat kindergarten in a regular classroom with an aide the next year. Things were about to change. But never, in my wildest imagination, could I have anticipated what was to come.

My son loved school and he was a joy to everyone who was exposed to him. He was an auditory learner because of his eyesight, so most of everything was read to him and explained to him by his aide. Getting a plan in order for school was a tiring, and sometimes frustrating, process, because he was somewhat of a pioneer in our school system. Still, the teachers were eager to provide him any help he needed in those early years, and I watched him flourish and grow.

A funny story — sort of. Matt sometimes had trouble distinguishing fantasy from reality. One time at school, he was playing like he was Superman and took a dive off of a loft 8 feet off the ground. Sometimes this one issue was quite a challenge for all of us! The goose-egg on his head gave us all quite a scare.

Hospitalizations became fewer and the seizures were fewer and farther between. With each year, he seemed to become stronger physically and socially. He was finally putting on weight, making friends, and seemed genuinely happy. He still had occasional seizures and still was sick quite a bit.

The medical community said he "may have" outgrown his seizures, that his brain (the 20% that was not damaged – come on!) had compensated for the damage, and although it would never be repaired, it would never be any worse. I believe differently, however. We'll get to that at the end of the story.

Although delighted with my son's progress I continued to feel horribly guilty as I was convinced his "condition" was my fault. I also felt so cheated and resentful – not of him – but of our life. Who else had a life like this? Why did this happen to me, to us? Why couldn't I have just had a normal life? Oh I remember: *"she doesn't stand a chance, she'll never amount to anything."* I was absolutely convinced this was exactly what I deserved, that it was strangely "right," but I was mad because my innocent son didn't deserve this. He would have been so much better off if he had been born to someone else! What was God thinking?

We had made a nice little life for ourselves in North Alabama although I hated it there. MY plan was that as soon as the present school year finished, I was going back to Tennessee. As so often in my life, my plans never materialized. Another reason to be mad and unhappy, and I was determined I would endure, do the best I could but I didn't want to be here so I was not going to be happy.

I had been taking my son to church since he was five, because I wanted to be a good parent. I wanted him to know about Jesus, so I did the proper parently thing: I took him to church, sometimes dropping him off and picking him up. I sometimes went, too, but felt very uncomfortable, regardless of where we went, because of my lifestyle. When I had free time when my son visited his dad (which was every other weekend) my lifestyle had not changed at all. I was still bound and determined to do what I wanted to do, with whom I wanted to do it, regardless of what anybody said or thought. You can imagine how totally miserable I was on Sunday mornings I went to church, sitting there, lost as a ball in high weeds. I had no direction, no plan or purpose for my life other than just to get through it. Of course, all the bitterness and resentment that accompanied the fact that nothing, *not one single thing*, had gone as I had planned.

At the time, I couldn't understand why God didn't allow me to have things the way I wanted them if He *really* loved me, as the preachers I listened to so adamantly promised. I mean, if He did (really love me), He'd want me to be happy, right?! Well, I wasn't happy, so apparently, He didn't love me and I surmised that it was all a lie. Nothing was good or easy in my life and I had nothing I wanted. My life, I felt, was a total disaster, a joke, and a complete waste. Why had all the bad things happened? Why couldn't I just die and get it over with?

Battles were raging, still, inside of me. I remarried (another chapter of the book of my life, to say the least). I thought he was my knight in shining armor. I thought he was heaven sent to save me, but that, too, turned ugly in just a very short time. When he left me, a friend of mine who was also Matt's sitter started hounding me about going to church. Every day, many times a day she talked about Jesus. "*Your life is poop, because you need Jesus...you need the Lord...come to church...come to church*" so one Wednesday night I did. I made her make a promise to me that, if I didn't like it, she wouldn't say another word to me. She promised, so I reluctantly went thinking "this will shut her up."

THE LOST GIRL IS FOUND

The pastor on that Wednesday night was talking absolutely, directly to me. It was like he and I were friends, a friend with whom I had entrusted with my life's story and he blabbed it to everyone! Suddenly, everything became crystal clear. Everything that had happened to me in the past 10 years, even the way I had grown up, suddenly finally made sense. All of it was to bring me to this moment in time. Everything had happened to bring me to my knees and to bring me to my Savior. I was on my Damascus road, not persecuting Christians, but persecuting myself, tormented and lost, and I had been blinded by the Light of Christ.

I accepted Christ that night as my Savior and suddenly I felt as though the weight of the world had been lifted off my shoulders and that heavy weight in my chest from my broken heart was gone. I could breathe! Everything was clear, for what I'm sure was the first time in my life.

I went to another church that my friend led me to because of a teacher she knew who would minister to me. From that point in my life my attitude about life and the things that had happened, entirely changed. For the first time, I had a clearer perspective of what life was all about. I had a purpose and, for the very first time, a sense of self-worth. For the first time in my life, I was LIVING instead of just existing. And that was just the beginning.

LIFE WORTH LIVING

When I got saved, not only did my perspective change, everything changed. I started seeing God at work in my son's life as well. My circumstances hadn't changed but I will say, everything we needed God provided. It's now 23 years since I got saved and I haven't had a drop of alcohol.

Miraculously, I also saw the manifestation of God's power through my son. We became involved in our church which, at that time, was fairly new and struggling. The pastor had just come a few months before I did, so we all were in for the experience of our lives and we didn't know it! The church literally took me and my son in despite my ugly past. I learned, through those wonderful people, who Jesus really is, and what He's capable of doing in a life that is totally surrendered to Him.

From the moment I became a Christian, everything seemed different. I often say the grass looked greener to me. I began to learn how to forgive myself and began to let go of and "unlearn" things I had believed about myself all of my life.

God deals with us and shows Himself to us just like we need Him to. He's so personal and interacts with us accordingly. I had so much self-hate and guilt over what had happened to my son at birth and he knew that. One day, I was driving listening to the radio to a preacher who said, "There's a mother listening who thinks her child's defects are totally her fault, and she has a huge weight of guilt because of that." He began to quote John 9:2-3: *"Rabbi, who sinned, this man or his parents, that he was born blind?"* Jesus answered, *"Neither this man nor his parents sinned,* **but that the works of God might be revealed in his life**.*"* (emphasis mine). At that moment, I started crying and felt a tremendous release from all that heavy guilt. I got out of my car, right there on I-65, and got on my knees thanking God for bringing that personal message to me. That's just one example of how personally He's dealt with me. I could go on and on.

After I was saved, Matt started thriving. He still had all the illnesses that any other child had, and when he had seizures, they were far less severe than what he had experienced in the past. Every year, I took him to North Carolina to have a series of tests done and every year, things remained pretty much the same – abnormal EEGs (brain wave tests), which indicated that he was having constant, ongoing seizure activity which was well controlled by the seizure medication he was on. He was, however, learning in school and progressing well, over and above our expectations.

His eyesight, however, was his major disability. He couldn't read well at all, yet when someone read to him, his comprehension level and language skills far surpassed children his age. Go figure that one; it doesn't make sense, does it? I choose to believe it was a "God thing."

During that time, I took him to a neuroophthalmologist in Birmingham, AL, for his visual problem and finally received an explanation about that. It wasn't a visual problem at all – it was a brain dysfunction problem. His brain would sometimes misconstrue the message to the eyes. He actually had 20/20 vision; it was the message that the eyes received from the brain that was so messed up. He also explained to me that the area of my son's brain that received the most intense damage was the part that controls muscle coordination and eyesight. So finally, after all these years, I understood why he had the problems he did. Sadly, he told us that there was nothing that could be done about his visual problems. His eyes crossed, fluctuated often when a lot of seizure activity was going on and so that meant that there was no hope of getting that problem fixed either, surgery would just be too risky and would be fruitless because of the constantly changing positions of his eyes due to the abnormal brain activity.

When he was 10 years old, we went to North Carolina for our usual round of tests and this time, the EEG was "improved" – still abnormal activity, but very much improved from the year prior. The next year, still improved, but he had a small seizure in PE one day which set us back for a week or so. He seemed to recover quickly and was very anxious to get back to school.

At age 11, he was ready to go to middle school, with his aide, and while there, I watched him blossom! He was reading by himself and looking up words in a large print dictionary – a first for him. There was that time, however, that he didn't want to look up his words. He made up his own definitions! So, that told us he had a very normal, very active reasoning capacity and imagination. As a matter of fact, I lost count of the meetings I had with his teachers, which I understand from other parents with "normal" children that age that all that was totally normal, too.

The boy was spreading his wings and becoming his own person, which included the associated trials of the adolescent experience, attitude, hormones raging, not always so pleasant and fun! All, I must say, brought me much joy and thankfulness. His neurologist told me that there was a battle going on inside of him. Tegretol (his seizure medication) versus testosterone. So use your imagination, or reflect back to when your child was growing up between the ages of 11-13 if applicable, and you will understand what we were going through. A challenge, to say the least.

I remember being so thankful that I was finally dealing with the *normal* issues and problems just like every other parent, and that we were no longer unique and in a battle that no one could relate to. It was nice, for a change, to experience a little normalcy!

When he was 12, I took him back to the eye doctor for a yearly checkup, who told us he wanted to perform nerve conduction studies on his eyes to see if there was any nerve damage. He had the studies done which showed very little activity in his left eye (the nerves feeding the information to his eye so he could actually see) was very slow and sporadic. The right eye study was "flat-lined" which means that the nerves in the right eye were not receiving any message at all from the nerves or brain, which meant that he was totally blind in his right eye.

Again, that hurt and anger enveloped me, as well as such sadness. My heart broke for him and again I felt so responsible. I felt that everything that had happened to him was totally

But Grace Prevailed

my fault. Needless to say, that was a very long, very painful trip back home. We stopped at Wal-Mart to pay out a lay away and, while standing in line, my son noticed a little boy playing with a kaleidoscope and asked me what that was. I told him after we got finished at lay-away, we would go to the toy department and I would show him.

To this day (this has now been 18 years ago), I think about that moment, and I still cry. My heart starts beating faster. We found a kaleidoscope and he put it up to his RIGHT eye (the blind eye, remember) and held it there for a couple of seconds. I told him to switch it to his left eye so he could see it. He said, "I can see it, Mom." Time seemed to stand still. I couldn't breathe. I asked, "You can *see*?" I asked him to describe what he was seeing, and then very carefully hand it to me so I could see it, too. He described, in great detail, all the colors he saw (purple, red, white, and yellow), the shape (a snow flake), and how beautiful it was. Then he handed it to me. He had described it perfectly. HE COULD SEE OUT OF HIS RIGHT EYE! I was so excited. I got down on my knees right there, in the Wal-Mart, in front of God and everybody, crying and thanking God for what I knew was another miracle. Beyond my wildest expectations. Over and beyond anything for which I could have asked. He could see out of his right eye.

We went straight home and I called the eye doctor's office and told them we had an emergency and we had to see the doctor as soon as possible.

"No eye has seen, nor ear has heard, no mind has conceived what God has prepared for those who love Him" 1st Corinthians 2:9. AMEN!

Two days later, we drove back down to Birmingham and the doctor examined my son, and examined him again. He reviewed his chart without saying a word, and let him read, with his right eye, an eye chart that, two days previously, he couldn't even see the large objects and letters on. He read the whole thing, even the small letters! He then said very quietly that he had "no medical explanation for this." My son, grinning from ear to ear, said, "I know what did it. It was God, wasn't it, Mommy?"

But Grace Prevailed

We praised and thanked God all the way back to Athens. You may think I'm crazy, you or may think this story is fictional, but I promise you, it's true. The next Sunday, I shared that with the members of my Sunday school class. And, of course, since all of us were women, we cried. I know in my heart we witnessed this miracle because of all the prayers of these wonderful people who had surrounded us with so much love.

That eye healing was just the beginning. A year or so after that, my son had eye muscle surgery (on those muscles of his eyes that the doctor had said that couldn't be surgically corrected, remember?) His eyesight has improved 100% - he now reads – READS at a remarkable level. He was totally independent at his school by the time he was in the 12th grade.

As further evidence of God's hands on my son's life, to date, it has been more than 13 years since he has had a seizure and he's off all his medications. He's worked for Cracker Barrel for almost 10 years now.

I promised the Lord that I would write this story after he finished high school. So, as I write this, I have wept many tears. My heart and mind have been reamed from one emotion to another. Contained in this book are just a few of the many, many ways our lives have been forever altered by the grace of God.

The Lord provided for every need. Even what I didn't know we needed, He provided. I was hired by the local hospital as a Medical Transcriptionist (I had no experience and was trained on the job) which would later allow me to work at home. As Matt got older that was a huge blessing. As a work-at-home Mom, I was allowed to be involved with all school activities, one of which included Special Olympics. Through a competition at the State Finals in Tuscaloosa, Matt got to meet his favorite musician at the time, Garth Brooks. He was also in Karate while in school, and earned a Black belt. Quite the accomplishment for a person that everyone had written off.

Because Matt lives with me and I work at home, this allows him to have lots of choices and freedoms. For instance, he can choose what shift he likes at work, what activities he wants to be involved in and my work allows me to work around his plans. That's important to me as I want him to have opportunities to make his own choices, just like everyone else.

Sometimes, it is good to step back and reflect on where you have been, what God brought you from and what He has done in your life. If you haven't done that lately, I would encourage you to do so.

Praise Him for where you are right now! I made God a solemn promise that I would, with every opportunity, share this amazing story to everyone and anyone who asked. I feel somewhat like the apostles who walked the streets with Jesus while He ministered as a man. I have seen the Lord. The Teacher has not only taken up residence in my heart and become the Lord of my life, but He has physically manifested Himself at my house. He has placed His mighty, healing hands on my precious baby boy, the one whom everyone thought was as good as dead, and He has given us life. And not just life—*life worth living with a hope and a future.*

"I will extol You, my God, O King; and I will bless Your name forever and ever. Every day, I will bless You, and I will praise Your name forever and ever. Great is the Lord and greatly to be praised; and His greatness is unsearchable" Psalm 145:1-3

As I complete this story to put in book form, Matt is 30 years old. I've had the privilege of seeing him grow into the wonderful, healthy person he is. I had the blessing of leading him to the Lord which was more of a gift than I can describe. As I did, I remember holding that baby up in his punkin seat and begging God just to let him live and take care of him because I could do nothing for him.

Life has been far from easy. But, oh my, what a life it has been. We've survived many heartbreaking things including the loss of my Mom and my sister whom Matt called "Honey." Mom didn't live to see me saved and I'm sorry about that. I was such a wounded person. I wish she could've shared the changes Jesus has made in my life. She worried so about me and her precious grandson. I think about her often, and wish she were here. Somehow, I think she's aware of what's happening with us. I can't wait to talk to her about all of this when I see her again in heaven.

Matt and I have done this life thing pretty much on our own with God seeing to us every step of the way. My family, with the exception of Mom, Mom's side of the family, Joy (my sister who we lost six years ago) has been distant to say the least. That's another story for another time. Looking back, had they been more involved with us, I might have missed what I know was God helping us and providing for us, every step of the way. I wouldn't have had it any other way.

This journey has been long and hard, gut-wrenching and heartbreaking, but it has also been the highlight of my life. I know, without a shadow of a doubt, that all the good and comprehension-defying things that have taken place in my son's life can only be of Christ. There is simply no other explanation.

I'll leave you with these thoughts:

If you find yourself hopeless with nothing but regret for things you've done and what's been done to you, give yourself to God. He can take your broken heart, broken dreams and broken soul and make a brand-new person out of you if you'll let Him. He can change a "nothing" into a "something." He makes it possible for us to forgive ourselves. I don't think that's possible in our own strength. I know it wasn't possible for me until I met Him. Nothing is impossible for God. No one, no matter how vile, self-hating and rebellious, is beyond His reach. If He saved me, He certainly can save anyone else.

If you find yourself with a sick baby, for whom no one has hope; if they tell you that nothing more can be done, lift that baby to the Lord! That humble act of reaching for Him has made all the difference in our lives. He did it for us; He definitely can do it for you!

As long as I live, I will never understand why God has blessed us so much. Even if my son had lived and never said a word, never taken a step, never smiled a smile, or worse yet, if he had died, I still would have mothered him the best that I could. I know, though, that the turning point in his life was the same turning point in my life: when I gave us both to Jesus. After all, I just asked that he live and now look! We, alone, cannot even comprehend or touch what God is capable of doing with a surrendered life. Take whatever you suffer with to the One who can do something about it no matter what *it* is!

You don't have to suffer the pain of taking the "long way around" as I did. He has made ALL the difference in my once barren life and the life of my son, and I can't wait to see what He chooses to do next! All of the glory goes to God.

I still look at that 30-year-old man and every single day, thank God for letting me have him this long. If it all ends tomorrow, we have already had more time than anyone thought we would. We have been blessed to see things in our lives that most can only dream (or read) about. We have had a very Personal Touch from the Master's Hand, a touch that cannot be explained or reasoned out. I've decided that His plan is a kazillion times more wonderful than mine, and I'm going for it!

*"...I have learned in whatever state I am, to be content: I know how to be abased, and I know how to abound. Everywhere and in all things, I have learned both to be full and to be hungry, both to abound and to suffer need. **I can do all things through Christ who strengthens me**"* Philippians 4:11-13

TO BE CONTINUED...

www.ingramcontent.com/pod-product-compliance
Lightning Source LLC
Chambersburg PA
CBHW070551050426
42450CB00011B/2819